THE CHRISTIAN DESERTION OF JESUS

HOW POLITICS, SOCIAL MEDIA, AND WORLDLY-MINDEDNESS HAVE BECOME A SUBSTITUTE FOR THE HOLY SPIRIT OF GOD IN THE CHURCH

DON MORGAN

New Harbor Press
RAPID CITY, SD

Morgan/New Harbor Press
1601 Mt. Rushmore Rd, Ste 3288
Rapid City, SD 57701
www.NewHarborPress.com

The Christian Desertion of Jesus / Don Morgan. —1st ed.
ISBN 978-1-63357-406-9

CONTENTS

To my friends in the UPC

IN THESE MODERN TIMES, the word *virgin* has become a dirty word. Christian boys and girls are not taught that Jesus expects them to be virgins when they marry. A multitude of preachers are making a lot of noise about the subject of abortion—but they are strangely silent on the subject of virginity. The virginally quiet pulpiteers are all the more puzzling—when one considers the fact that the Gospel of Jesus Christ began with a young woman who was a virgin. Many Bible sermonizers have abandoned Jesus for a cheapened, socially popular religion.

PREFACE

Redeeming the time, because the days are evil.
Ephesians 5:16

YOUR TIME ON EARTH IS a precious gift to you from God. He created you, and He continually creates for you—every second, minute, hour, day, week, month, and year that you breathe on this planet. Time, as God created it, is a holy thing. Time is spiritual silver and gold. Time is spiritual money. Time *is* precious.

Time is the spiritual foundation and the physical support of your life. Anything that you accomplish for God you do it utilizing the time that He gives you. Using God's time, you can become a pastor, preacher, evangelist, seminary professor, or world traveling missionary. With God's time in your hands, you can become an exceptional husband or wife, father or mother, or an excellent mentor or spiritual parent to someone.

Within God's framework of time, you can become a butcher, a baker, a candlestick maker, a doctor, a lawyer, a liar, or a thief.

Many people in these modern times are spiritual thieves. Instead of giving God a true tithe of their time, they squander away His precious moments on things that are not sanctioned by His Spirit.

Foremost among the things that Christians misspend time on are politics, social media, and run-of-the-mill worldly-mindedness (vain TV shows, ungodly movies, music, games, entertainment, etc.)

Politics and worldly-minded politicians would be valuable for ten thousand times ten thousand years, if they taught people to live these ten words of Jesus on the cross:

> *Father, forgive them; for they know not what they do.*
> (Luke 23:34)

As it is, politics and politicians *will not* teach these ten words. It is what it is.

There are social media platforms that increase their profits by allowing Scripture to be taught. But the words of the preachers and their Bible teachings are drowned out by an ungodly flood of babble—and the attractive lies of the Serpent. Young people who use social media for their daily Bible bread usually wade through a cesspool of devil-dung, before and after the Scriptural lessons. Their minds become a house divided.

> *And he called them unto him, and said unto them in parables, How can Satan cast out Satan? ²⁴And if a kingdom be divided against itself, that kingdom cannot stand. ²⁵And if a house be divided against itself, that house cannot stand.*
> (Mark 3:23–25)

There are more cell phones than print Bibles in many congregations these days. Church people say they are reading Bible apps on the phone, but the reality is they are a divided house that is sharing a platform with friends of the devil while attending a Sunday assembly that is dedicated to Jesus.

Don't team up with those who are unbelievers. How can righteousness be a partner with wickedness? How can light live with darkness? ¹⁵ What harmony can there be between Christ and the devil? How can a believer be a partner with an unbeliever? ¹⁶ And what union can there be between God's temple and idols? For we are the temple of the living God. As God said: "I will live in them and walk among them. I will be their God, and they will be my people. ¹⁷ Therefore, come out from among unbelievers, and separate yourselves from them, says the Lord. Don't touch their filthy things, and I will welcome you. ¹⁸ And I will be your Father, and you will be my sons and daughters, says the Lord Almighty." (2 Corinthians 6:14–18 NLT)

Amish Christians deliberately repudiate many modern time saving conveniences and spend more time working with their hands for the basic necessities of life. They say it pushes them closer to heaven. The vast majority of their time is spent on things approved by God.

God's purpose for your life time is for you to demonstrate His everlasting holiness to the temporal world. But you *must invest a considerable amount of time learning about the God of the Holy Bible* in order to fulfil His plan for your life.

The New Testament is composed of 260 chapters, 7,959 verses, and 184,000 words. If a person read one chapter a day, he or she could finish the entire book in less than a year. The Scriptures prescribe self-study:

Study to shew thyself approved unto God, a workman that needeth not to be ashamed, rightly dividing the word of truth. (2 Timothy 2:15)

The Bible also directs the king of the nation to study the Holy Scriptures:

> *And it shall be, when he sitteth upon the throne of his king-dom, that he shall write him a copy of this law in a book out of that which is before the priests, the Levites:* [19] *And it shall be with him, and* **he shall read therein all the days of his life***: that he may learn to fear the LORD his God, to keep all the words of this law and these statutes, to do them:* [20] *That his heart be not lifted up above his brethren, and that he turn not aside from the commandment, to the right hand, or to the left: to the end that he may prolong his days in his kingdom, he, and his children, in the midst of Israel.*
> (Deuteronomy 17:18–20)

God has instructed everyone from kings to presidents, politicians, peasants and paupers to bow their heads in the reverent study of His Word.

> *I will study your commandments and reflect on your ways.*
> [16] *I will delight in your decrees and not forget your word.*
> (Psalm 119:15–16 NLT)

Unfortunately, among church people and worldly people alike *more heads are bowed over cell phone posts on Facebook*, Snapchat, Twitter, YouTube, Instagram, TikTok, and Spotify in one day than those who seriously study the Bible in one year. The price that is being paid for the substitution of the Words of the Bible for the words of social media is the desertion of Jesus Christ.

> *Their land is full of idols; the* **people worship things they have made with their own hands.** (Isaiah 2:8 NLT)

The Super-Politician, the Antichrist, will rise to power and influence within the dark social setting of Facebook religion. Social media pulpits will be the main method of the communication of his messages. Evangelists and Evangelical groups will swallow the lies of the Antichrist hook, line and sinker. He will cause the Evangelicals to believe that he is the Champion of Israel. He will claim that his political brilliance—not God's Providence—has established Jerusalem as the spiritual capital of the world. He will be trusted. Jesus Christ will be abandoned for political expediency *and* Barabbas the murderer (a foretoken of the Antichrist).

Barabbas' full name was *Jesus* Barabbas. Just as the religious authorities rejected the holy Jesus Christ for the unholy thief Jesus Barabbas, the Evangelical authorities will reject the true Spirit of Christ for the time-stealing spirit of the Antichrist (see John 18:39–40, Matthew 27:20–26, and Mark 15:6–13).

Just as it was the mission of Jesus of Nazareth to reveal the attributes of God His Father to the visible world (see John 14:7–11), it is the mission of the Church of Jesus to shine forth the character of Christ in a darkening social environment.

The Bible tells us—as members of the Kingdom of God—we are the servants of Christ. And that it is our privilege to serve people the righteousness, peace, and the joy of the Holy Spirit (see Romans 14:17–18). We are also taught by Scripture to *first give God our bodies by making them holy*, and then let Him transform our minds:

> *And so, dear brothers and sisters, I plead with you to give your bodies to God because of all he has done for you. Let them be a living and holy sacrifice—the kind he will find acceptable. This is truly the way to worship him.* [2] *Don't copy the behavior and customs of this world, but let God transform you into a new person by changing the way you think. Then you will learn to know God's will for you, which is good and pleasing and perfect.* (Romans 12:1–2 NLT)

If Christians would obey the Word of God by serving humanity the righteousness, peace, and the joy of the Spirit, the church would be a powerful force for good in the world. It doesn't take a lot of observation for one to see that the righteousness, peace, and the joy of God is fast disappearing from a multitude of churches.

Many churches are not houses of healing—that is, spiritual dispensaries of the healing balm of God's righteousness, peace, and joy. Instead, they have become entertainment venues or places where people are encouraged to fight for political purposes. Fighting for political victories has replaced striving for the peace of God in many congregations.

A person cannot give something that he or she does not have. Likewise, if a church does not have righteousness, peace, and joy, it cannot give righteousness, peace, and joy to anyone. But it can *substitute* worldly-minded protests for righteousness, politics for peace, and entertainment for the joy of the Holy Spirit of God.

Because politics, social media, and worldly-mindedness are so dominant in congregations today, rare is the congregant who has any concept of what the term *Holy* in the "Holy Spirit of God" means.

> *Because we have these promises* [from God], *dear friends, let us cleanse ourselves from everything that can defile our body or spirit. And **let us work toward complete holiness** because we fear God.* (2 Corinthians 7:1 NLT)

> *But as He who called you is holy, you also be holy in all your conduct,* [16] *because it is written, "Be holy, for I am holy."* (1 Peter 1:15–16 NKJV)

A worldly-minded man cannot be holy because he does not have the Holy Spirit of God directing his conscience. A worldly-minded congregation also cannot be holy because it does not have God's Holy Spirit setting the direction of the church. Such a church will invariably abandon the Faith of Jesus—and follow the dictates of the devil.

*Now the Spirit speaketh expressly, that **in the latter times some shall depart from the faith, giving heed to seducing spirits, and doctrines of devils;*** [2] *Speaking lies in hypocrisy; having their conscience seared with a hot iron.* (1 Timothy 4:1–2)

[1]

CHILDREN MUST BE TAUGHT BY THEIR PARENTS TO VALUE GOD'S HOLINESS

For I was born a sinner—yes, from the moment my mother conceived me.
Psalm 51:5 (NLT)

ONLY IN THE SEXLESS BIRTH of Jesus Christ do we find a person who was born holy. The rest of us were born with the innate sin nature that we inherited from the original sinners—Adam and Eve.

> Just as everyone dies because we all belong to Adam, everyone who belongs to Christ will be given new life. (1 Corinthians 15:22 NLT)

Even Jesus had to learn of God—and grow into higher and higher degrees of holiness:

Even though Jesus was God's Son, he learned obedience from the things he suffered. (Hebrews 5:8 NLT)

Jesus was taught by His earthly parents—Joseph and Mary—to participate in the Jewish festivals of their faith (see Luke 2:41–42). His earthly parents also instilled in Him the habit of attending the synagogue every Sabbath day and reading the Holy Scriptures:

When he [Jesus] came to the village of Nazareth, his boyhood home, he went as usual to the synagogue on the Sabbath and stood up to read the Scriptures. (Luke 4:16 NLT)

Jesus, like Joseph His earthly father, was a carpenter (see Matthew 13:53–56):

The next Sabbath he began teaching in the synagogue, and many who heard him were amazed. They asked, "Where did he get all this wisdom and the power to perform such miracles?" [3] *Then they scoffed, "He's just a carpenter, the son of Mary and the brother of James, Joseph, Judas, and Simon. And his sisters live right here among us." They were deeply offended and refused to believe in him.* (Mark 6:2–3 NLT)

Jesus worked as a carpenter until He was thirty years old. At the age of thirty, He was baptized by John the Baptist—and the Holy Spirit of God came to live inside His heart (see Luke 3:21–23).

When the Holy Spirit entered the heart of Jesus, He was transformed from a holy man who was obedient to the teachings of His parents to the Christ—the Anointed One, the Messiah of God. In a sense, the Spirit of God was previously welcomed into His mind through the discipleship of His earthly parents. When God the Father entered His heart—Jesus would then say, "I and my Father are one" (see John 10:30).

The example in the life of Christ—the earthly parents teaching the child about God until the child is transformed by a "new birth"— is God's pattern for you and your children. The Bible strongly admonishes parents to cling to God's words—and teach them to their children:

> *So commit yourselves wholeheartedly to these words of mine. Tie them to your hands and wear them on your forehead as reminders. 19 **Teach them to your children.** Talk about them when you are at home and when you are on the road, when you are going to bed and when you are getting up. 20 Write them on the doorposts of your house and on your gates, 21 so that as long as the sky remains above the earth, you and your children may flourish in the land the Lord swore to give your ancestors.* (Deuteronomy 11:18–21 NLT)

God wants you to love His Words and teach your children to love them. The book of Deuteronomy speaks of the bountiful blessings that would come to the Israelites if they learned to obey His directives:

> *If you fully obey the Lord your God and carefully keep all his commands that I am giving you today, the Lord your God will set you high above all the nations of the world. 2 You will experience all these blessings if you obey the Lord your God: 3 Your towns and your fields will be blessed. 4 Your children and your crops will be blessed. The offspring of your herds and flocks will be blessed. 5 Your fruit baskets and breadboards will be blessed. 6 Wherever you go and whatever you do, you will be blessed. 7 The Lord will con-*

quer your enemies when they attack you. They will attack you from one direction, but they will scatter from you in seven! ⁸ The Lord will guarantee a blessing on everything you do and will fill your storehouses with grain. The Lord your God will bless you in the land he is giving you. ⁹ If you obey the commands of the Lord your God and walk in his ways, the Lord will establish you as his holy people as he swore he would do.¹⁰ Then all the nations of the world will see that you are a people claimed by the Lord, and they will stand in awe of you. ¹¹ The Lord will give you prosperity in the land he swore to your ancestors to give you, blessing you with many children, numerous livestock, and abundant crops. (Deuteronomy 28:1–11 NLT)

Deuteronomy also speaks of the curses that would overtake the people of Israel if they ignored God's commandments or refused to obey Him:

But if you refuse to listen to the Lord your God and do not obey all the commands and decrees I am giving you today, all these curses will come and overwhelm you: ¹⁶ Your towns and your fields will be cursed. ¹⁷ Your fruit baskets and breadboards will be cursed. ¹⁸ Your children and your crops will be cursed. The offspring of your herds and flocks will be cursed. ¹⁹ Wherever you go and whatever you do, you will be cursed. ²⁰ The Lord himself will send on you curses, confusion, and frustration in everything you do, until at last you are completely destroyed for doing evil and abandoning me. ²¹ The Lord will afflict you with diseases until none of you are left in the land you are about to enter and occupy. ²² The Lord will strike you with wasting diseases, fever, and inflammation, with scorching heat and drought, and with blight and mildew. These disasters will pursue you until you die. ²³ *The skies above will be as unyielding as bronze, and the earth beneath will be as hard as iron.* ²⁴ *The Lord will change the rain that falls on your land into powder, and dust will pour down from the sky until you are destroyed.* ²⁵ *The Lord will cause you to be defeated by your enemies. You will attack your enemies from one direction, but you will scatter from them in seven! You will be an object of horror to all the kingdoms of the earth.* (Deuteronomy 28:15–25 NLT)

If you know the history of God's chosen people, the nation of Israel (see Exodus 19:5–6), then you probably know that time after time they rejected His words. King Zedekiah was the last ruler in Jerusalem when one of the Seven Wonders of the Ancient World—King Solomon's Temple of the Lord—was destroyed by the Babylonians:

Zedekiah was twenty-one years old when he became king, and he reigned in Jerusalem eleven years. ¹² *He did what was evil in the sight of the Lord his God, and he refused to humble himself when the prophet Jeremiah spoke to him directly from the Lord.* ¹³ *He also rebelled against King Nebuchadnezzar, even though he had taken an oath of loyalty in God's name. Zedekiah was a hard and stubborn man, refusing to turn to the Lord, the God of Israel.* ¹⁴ *Likewise, all the leaders of the priests and the people became more and more unfaithful. They followed all the pagan practices of the surrounding nations, desecrating the Temple of the Lord that had been consecrated in Jerusalem.* ¹⁵ *The Lord, the God of their ancestors, repeatedly sent his prophets to warn them, for he had compassion on his people and his Temple.* ¹⁶ *But the people mocked these messengers of God and despised their words. They scoffed at the prophets until the Lord's anger could no longer be restrained and nothing could be done. [17] So the Lord brought the king of Babylon against them. The Babylonians killed Judah's young men, even chasing after them into the Temple. They had no pity on the people, killing both young men and young women, the old and the infirm. God handed all of them over to Nebuchadnezzar. [18] The king took home to Babylon all the articles, large and small, used in the Temple of God, and the treasures from both the Lord's Temple and from the palace of the king and his officials. [19] Then his army burned the Temple of God, tore down the walls of Jerusalem, burned all the palaces, and completely destroyed everything of value. [20] The few who survived were taken as exiles to Babylon, and they became servants to the king and his sons until the kingdom of Persia came to power.* (2 Chronicles 36:11–20 NLT)

The Temple of the Lord and the walls of Jerusalem were destroyed at the end of the reign of Zedekiah. King Zedekiah was one of the many political rulers in Israel who set the example of ignoring the Word of God. Other kings instituted idolatrous worship practices—instead of worshipping the Lord God of their ancestors—Abraham, Isaac, Jacob, and Moses.

King Jeroboam introduced calf worship (see 1 Kings 12:26–33). King Ahab and his queen Jezebel instituted to worship of the pagan god Baal and the fertility goddess Asherah (see 1 Kings 16:30–33). Shrines to the goddess Asherah are called *groves* in the King James Version of the Bible.

And Ahab made a grove; and Ahab did more to provoke the LORD God of Israel to anger than all the kings of Israel that were before him. (1 Kings 16:33)

Worse, he [Ahab] *went on and built a shrine to the sacred whore Asherah. He made the God of Israel angrier than all the previous kings of Israel put together.* (1 Kings 16:33 MSG)

The worship of Asherah—Jezebel's goddess—included phallic symbols (*Asherah poles*), sex rites, and shrine prostitutes. It is interesting that 800 years after Jezebel's death, the resurrected Jesus complains about her presence in His church (see Revelation 2:20–21).

Ahab and Jezebel made the city of Samaria the headquarters of heathen worship in Northern Israel. They worshipped golden calves, they worshipped Baal and Asherah, they practiced witchcraft, and they sacrificed their newborn children to pagan gods by burning them on fire altars:

They rejected all the commands of the Lord their God and made two calves from metal. They set up an Asherah pole and worshiped Baal and all the forces of heaven. ¹⁷ *They even sacrificed their own sons and daughters in the fire. They consulted fortune-tellers and practiced sorcery and sold themselves to evil, arousing the Lord's anger.* (2 Kings 17:16–17 NLT)

One of the worst kings of Southern Israel was King Manasseh. Jewish tradition tells it was Manasseh who killed the prophet Isaiah—by having him sawn in half. King Manasseh was a murderer and an idolater who desecrated the Temple of the Lord in Jerusalem. He also burned his own children on fire altars as sacrifices to profane gods:

Manasseh also murdered many innocent people until Jerusalem was filled from one end to the other with innocent blood. This was in addition to the sin that he caused the people of Judah to commit, leading them to do evil in the Lord's sight. (2 Kings 21:16 NLT)

Manasseh was twelve years old when he became king, and he reigned in Jerusalem fifty-five years. [2] *He did what was evil in the Lord's sight, following the detestable practices of the pagan nations that the Lord had driven from the land ahead of the Israelites.* [3] *He rebuilt the pagan shrines his father, Hezekiah, had broken down. He constructed altars for the images of Baal and set up Asherah poles. He also bowed before all the powers of the heavens and worshiped them.* [4] *He built pagan altars in the Temple of the Lord, the place where the Lord had said, "My name will remain in Jerusalem forever."* [5] *He built these altars for all the powers of the heavens* [Manasseh built an altar to the star god Chiun (Saturn)—see Amos 5:26] *and altars to other false gods in both courtyards of the Lord's Temple.* [6] *Manasseh also sacrificed his own sons in the fire in the valley of Ben-Hinnom. He practiced sorcery, divination, and witchcraft, and he consulted with mediums and psychics. He did much that was evil in the Lord's sight, arousing his anger.*

[7] *Manasseh even took a carved idol he had made and set it up in God's Temple, the very place where God had told David and his son Solomon: "My name will be honored forever in this Temple and in Jerusalem—the city I have chosen from among all the tribes of Israel.* [8] *If the Israelites will be careful to obey my commands—all the laws, decrees, and regulations given through Moses—I will not send them into exile from this land that I set aside for your ancestors."* [9] *But Manasseh led the people of Judah and Jerusalem to do even more evil than the pagan nations that the Lord had*

destroyed when the people of Israel entered the land. ¹⁰ *The Lord spoke to Manasseh and his people, but they ignored all his warnings.* (2 Chronicles 33:1–10 NLT)

King Manasseh brought his nation to a lower level of debauchery by sacrificing his own children to demonic pagan gods. The example of infanticide that he set was followed by the residents of the country. The Bible says they "sacrificed their sons and their daughters unto devils."

> *Yea,* **they sacrificed their sons and their daughters unto devils,** ³⁸ **And shed innocent blood, even the blood of their sons and of their daughters, whom they sacrificed unto the idols of Canaan**: *and the land was polluted with blood.* ³⁹ *Thus were they defiled with their own works, and went a whoring with their own inventions.* ⁴⁰ *Therefore was the wrath of the LORD kindled against his people, insomuch that he abhorred his own inheritance.* ⁴¹ *And he gave them into the hand of the heathen; and they that hated them ruled over them.* ⁴² *Their enemies also oppressed them, and they were brought into subjection under their hand.* (Psalm 106:37–42)

The Israelites deserted the Lord. Instead of teaching their children reverence to the Holy God of Israel, <u>the kings and the people gave their children to the idols of the Devil</u>. This sin against their own children is the reason Solomon's Temple was destroyed—and the Israelites were exiled to other nations of the world. The Israeli failure to instill God's Law in children, plus the sin of later rejecting Jesus Christ, is the reason Jews are hated all over the world today.

And I will cause them to be removed into all kingdoms of the earth, because of Manasseh the son of Hezekiah king of Judah, for that which he did in Jerusalem. (Jeremiah 15:4)

Pilate saith unto them, What shall I do then with Jesus which is called Christ? They all say unto him, Let him be crucified. 23 *And the governor said, Why, what evil hath he done? But they cried out the more, saying, Let him be crucified.* 24 *When Pilate saw that he could prevail nothing, but that rather a tumult was made, he took water, and washed his hands before the multitude, saying, I am innocent of the blood of this just person: see ye to it.* 25 *Then answered all the people, and said,* **His blood be on us, and on our children.** (Matthew 27:22–25)

History repeats itself (see Ecclesiastes 1:9 and 3:15). The old nation of Israel (that was based on the Old Testament) refused to teach their children about the true holiness of God. Instead, **they *literally* gave their children to the *idols* of the Devil:**

Then you took your sons and daughters—the children you had borne to me—and sacrificed them to your gods. Was your prostitution not enough? 21 *Must you also slaughter my children by sacrificing them to idols?* (Ezekiel 16:20–21 NLT)

They have committed both adultery and murder—adultery by worshiping idols and murder by burning as sacrifices the children they bore to me. 38 *Furthermore, they have defiled my Temple and violated my Sabbath day!* 39 **On the very day that they sacrificed their children to their idols, they boldly came into my Temple to worship! They came in and defiled my house.** (Ezekiel 23:37–39 NLT)

Likewise, the new nation of Israel (the church based on the New Testament—the Christian church) has mostly refused to teach their children about the true holiness of Jesus. Instead, the Church has abandoned Christ—and has *spiritually* **given her children to the *impious idols* of Facebook, Snapchat, Twitter, YouTube, Instagram, TikTok, and Spotify.**

THE CROSS OF CHRIST MEANS SUFFERING FOR JESUS

It is a faithful saying: For if we be dead with him, we shall also live with him: 12 *If we suffer, we shall also reign with him: if we deny him, he also will deny us.*
2 Timothy 2:11–12

YOU HAVE PROBABLY HEARD HUNDREDS of sermons about the suffering and death of Jesus on the cross—for your sins and the sins of the world. And you have probably heard sermons about Hebrews 13:8: Jesus is the same today as He was yesterday—and as He will be forever. With the idea in mind that Jesus is forever the same, does that in any way imply that His suffering will also continue forever? Yes and no. Yes, in the sense that you (the church) are the body of Jesus Christ (see 1 Corinthians 12:27)—and you will suffer for Him as long as you are in this Devil-dominated world.

*And since we are his children, we are his heirs. In fact, together with Christ we are heirs of God's glory. **But if we are to share his glory, we must also share his suffering.*** 18 *Yet*

25

what we suffer now is nothing compared to the glory he will reveal to us later.[19] *For all creation is waiting eagerly for that future day when God will reveal who his children really are.*[20] *Against its will, all creation was subjected to God's curse* [**because of the Serpent's lies in the Garden of Eden**]. *But with eager hope,* [21] *the creation looks forward to the day when it will join God's children in glorious freedom from death and decay.*[22] *For we know that all creation has been groaning as in the pains of childbirth right up to the present time.* [23] *And we believers also groan, even though we have the Holy Spirit within us as a foretaste of future glory, for we long for our bodies to be released from sin and suffering. We, too, wait with eager hope for the day when God will give us our full rights as his adopted children, including the new bodies he has promised us.* (Romans 8:17–23 NLT)

Be sober, be vigilant; because your adversary **the devil walks about like a roaring lion**, *seeking whom he may devour.* [9] *Resist him, steadfast in the faith, knowing that the same sufferings are experienced by your brotherhood in the world.* [10] *But may the God of all grace, who called us to His eternal glory by Christ Jesus,* **after you have suffered a while**, *perfect, establish, strengthen, and settle you.* (1 Peter 5:8–10 NKJV)

The sufferings of humanity will forever end the moment the Devil meets his doom in the lake of fire (see Revelation 20:10). The suffering of the body of Jesus (the church) will end when the Devil becomes toast—and a new heaven and a new earth is birthed forth from the volcanic detonation of Satan's incineration (see 2 Peter 3:10–13).

*And I saw a new heaven and a new earth: for the first heaven and the first earth were passed away; and there was no more sea. ² And I John saw the holy city, new Jerusalem, coming down from God out of heaven, prepared as a bride adorned for her husband. ³ And I heard a great voice out of heaven saying, Behold, the tabernacle of God is with men, and he will dwell with them, and they shall be his people, and God himself shall be with them, and be their God. ⁴ And **God shall wipe away all tears from their eyes; and there shall be no more death, neither sorrow, nor crying, neither shall there be any more pain**: for the former things are passed away. ⁵ And he that sat upon the throne said, Behold, I make all things new. And he said unto me, Write: for these words are true and faithful. (Revelation 21:1–5)*

Until the day the world no longer needs the light of the sun (see Revelation 21:23), Christians will suffer because of the spiritual warfare going on in the world (see Ephesians 6:11–12). The cross of Christ isn't a chain of gold and a piece of jewelry around one's neck, **it's a life that is chained to Jesus through thick and thin.**

The term *a servant of Jesus Christ* means "a *slave* of Jesus Christ" in the original Greek language of the Bible. New Testament slaves who were Christians were admonished to be obedient to their earthly masters—in all circumstances (see Ephesians 6:5–7 and 1 Peter 2:18–21).

Believers who owned slaves were taught to regard them as *temporary servants* and forever brothers.

He [Onesimus] is no longer like a slave to you. He is more than a slave, for he is a beloved brother, especially to me. Now he will mean much more to you, both as a man and as a brother in the Lord. (Philemon 1:16 NLT)

> *Masters, give unto your servants that which is just and equal; knowing that ye also have a Master in heaven.* (Colossians 4:1)

> *This letter is from Paul, **a slave of Christ Jesus**, chosen by God to be an apostle and sent out to preach his Good News.* (Romans 1:1 NLT)

God used the apostle Paul to write more New Testament letters than any other Apostle. Thousands of sermons are preached using the contents of Paul's letters to the churches. But I haven't heard one sermon preached using the following statement from Paul in his Epistle to the church at Colossae. I'm providing it here in two different versions of the Bible to help you to better understand what he is saying:

> *I now rejoice in my sufferings for you, and fill up in my flesh what is lacking in the afflictions of Christ, for the sake of His body, which is the church.* (Colossians 1:24 NKJV)

> *There's a lot of suffering to be entered into this world—the kind of suffering Christ takes on. I welcome the chance to take my share in the church's part of that suffering.* (Colossians 1:24 MSG)

The cross of Christ means suffering for Jesus. Suffering is an endemic part of the Christian life. A church that doesn't teach its members about the personal cross of suffering each disciple of Christ must bear is teaching a sterile, crossless Gospel.

The first perquisite for a person to be a disciple of Christ means that he or she must accept discipline *from* Christ. That is the Gospel the Epistle to the Hebrews proclaims:

*For **the Lord disciplines those he loves, and he punishes each one he accepts as his child**. [7] As you endure this divine discipline, remember that God is treating you as his own children. Who ever heard of a child who is never disciplined by its father? [8] If God doesn't discipline you as he does all of his children, it means that you are illegitimate and are not really his children at all . . . **God's discipline is always good for us**, so that we might share in his holiness. [11] **No discipline is enjoyable while it is happening—it's painful!** But afterward there will be a peaceful harvest of right living for those who are trained in this way.* (Hebrews 12:6–11 NLT)

Jesus said the purpose of His chastisement is to bring people to a state of repentance:

As many as I love, I rebuke and chasten: be zealous therefore, and repent. (Revelation 3:19)

The apostle Paul used the suffering he endured as verification that he truly was an Apostle of Christ—although he never saw Jesus in the flesh (see 2 Corinthians 13:3):

Are they Hebrews? So am I. Are they Israelites? So am I. Are they descendants of Abraham? So am I. [23] Are they servants of Christ? I know I sound like a madman, but I have served him far more! I have worked harder, been put in prison more often, been whipped times without number, and faced death again and again. [24] Five different times the Jewish leaders gave me thirty-nine lashes. [25] Three times I was beaten with rods. Once I was stoned. Three times I was shipwrecked. Once I spent a whole night and a day adrift at sea. [26] I have traveled on many long journeys. I have faced danger from rivers and from robbers. I have faced danger from my own people, the Jews, as well as from the Gentiles. I have faced danger in the cities, in the deserts, and on the seas. And I have faced danger from men who claim to be believers but are not. 27 I have worked hard and long, enduring many sleepless nights. I have been hungry and thirsty and have often gone without food. I have shivered in the cold, without enough clothing to keep me warm.28 Then, besides all this, I have the daily burden of my concern for all the churches. (2 Corinthians 11:22–28 NLT)

*As for me, may I never boast about anything except the cross of our Lord Jesus Christ. Because of that cross, my interest in this world has been crucified, and the world's interest in me has also died. . . . 17 From now on, don't let anyone trouble me with these things. For **I bear on my body the scars that show I belong to Jesus.*** (Galatians 6:14–17 NLT)

Paul said Jesus made him a minister of the Gospel—an example for the believers in Christ that would follow after him:

*This is a faithful saying, and worthy of all acceptation, that Christ Jesus came into the world to save sinners; of whom I am chief. 16 Howbeit for this cause I obtained mercy, that **in me first Jesus Christ might shew forth all longsuffering, for a pattern to them which should hereafter believe on him to life everlasting.*** (1 Timothy 1:15–16)

Paul encouraged Christians to follow his example—and he warned against "enemies of the cross of Christ."

*Dear brothers and sisters, **pattern your lives after mine**, and learn from those who follow our example.* [18] *For I have told you often before, and I say it again with tears in my eyes, that **there are many whose conduct shows they are really enemies of the cross of Christ**.* [19] *They are headed for destruction. Their god is their appetite, they brag about shameful things, <u>and they think only about this life here on earth</u>.* [20] *But we are citizens of heaven, where the Lord Jesus Christ lives. And we are eagerly waiting for him to return as our Savior.* (Philippians 3:17–20 NLT)

Churches that teach a Gospel of Prosperity are among those who are enemies of the cross of Christ. The cross of Christ means suffering for Jesus.

And he [Jesus] said to them all, If any man will come after me, let him deny himself, and take up his cross daily, and follow me. (Luke 9:23)

Through suffering, our bodies continue to share in the death of Jesus so that the life of Jesus may also be seen in our bodies. (2 Corinthians 4:10 NLT)

<u>Always bearing about in the body the dying of the Lord Jesus, that the life also of Jesus might be made manifest in our body</u>. (2 Corinthians 4:10)

[3]

Jesus Is the Bridegroom and the Church Is His Bride

The Kingdom of Heaven can be illustrated by the story of a king [God] *who prepared a great wedding feast for his son* [Jesus].

Matthew 22:2 (NLT)

THERE IS GOING TO BE a party that you don't want to miss. You have been invited to the Great Wedding Reception of the Ages—in Heaven:

> *Let us be glad and rejoice, and give honour to him: for the marriage of the Lamb* [Jesus] *is come, and his wife* [the church] *hath made herself ready.* [8] *And to her was granted that she should be arrayed in fine linen, clean and white: for the fine linen is the righteousness of saints.* [9] *And he saith unto me, Write, Blessed are they which are called unto the marriage supper* [the wedding reception] *of the Lamb. And he saith unto me, These are the true sayings of God.* (Revelation 19:7–9)

This wedding party takes place in heaven, but your engagement and marriage to Jesus the Bridegroom must happen in your heart and in your mind on earth. Then you must live your life in the world like a married woman who is waiting for her beloved husband to return from a long journey.

> *For the good man [Jesus] is not at home, he is gone a long journey:* [20] *He hath taken a bag of money [the riches of the kingdom of heaven] with him, and will come home at the day appointed.* (Proverbs 7:19–20)

> *And at midnight there was a cry made, Behold, the bridegroom cometh; go ye out to meet him.* (Matthew 25:6)

In Bible times, betrothal to a future husband was first arranged by an emissary (the groom's father or relative) bringing a proposal of marriage. If the maiden and her family accepted the engagement, she and the groom were married in the eyes of the law. Later, they would have a wedding ceremony, a wedding party, and conjoin in the marriage bed.

Joseph and the Virgin Mary had a typical biblical betrothal—until it was interrupted by the angel Gabriel:

> *In the sixth month of Elizabeth's pregnancy, God sent the angel Gabriel [Gabriel means: man of God] to Nazareth, a village in Galilee,* [27] *to a virgin named Mary. She was engaged to be married to a man named Joseph, a descendant of King David.* [28] *Gabriel appeared to her and said, "Greetings, favored woman! The Lord is with you!"* [29] *Confused and disturbed, Mary tried to think what the angel could mean.* [30] *"Don't be afraid, Mary," the angel told her, "for you have found favor with God!* [31] *You will conceive and give birth to a son, and you will name him Jesus.* [32] *He*

will be very great and will be called the Son of the Most High. The Lord God will give him the throne of his ancestor David. [33] And he will reign over Israel forever; his Kingdom will never end!" [34] Mary asked the angel, "But how can this happen? I am a virgin." [35] The angel replied, "The Holy Spirit will come upon you, and the power of the Most High will overshadow you. So the baby to be born will be holy, and he will be called the Son of God . . . [37] For nothing is impossible with God." [38] Mary responded, "I am the Lord's servant. May everything you have said about me come true." And then the angel left her. (Luke 1:26–38 NLT)

This is how Jesus the Messiah was born. His mother, Mary, was engaged to be married to Joseph. But before the marriage took place, while she was still a virgin, she became pregnant through the power of the Holy Spirit. [19] Joseph, her fiancé, was a good man and did not want to disgrace her publicly, so he decided to break the engagement quietly. [20] As he considered this, an angel of the Lord appeared to him in a dream. "Joseph, son of David," the angel said, "do not be afraid to take Mary as your wife. For the child within her was conceived by the Holy Spirit. [21] And she will have a son, and you are to name him Jesus, for he will save his people from their sins." [22] All of this occurred to fulfill the Lord's message through his prophet: [23] "Look! The virgin will conceive a child! She will give birth to a son, and they will call him Immanuel, which means 'God is with us.'" [24] When Joseph woke up, he did as the angel of the Lord commanded and took Mary as his wife. [25] But he did not have sexual relations with her until her son was born. And Joseph named him Jesus. (Matthew 1:18–25 NLT)

The story of the Virgin Mary and Gabriel is a foretelling of every person who accepts Jesus (the Word of God)—and becomes a Christian. Gabriel, the man of God, brought a message from the Lord to Mary. She accepted the messenger and his message and the Word from God impregnated her heart, mind, and womb with a New Life from heaven. The New Life grew inside her until Jesus Christ was born into the world. The Man Child (see Revelation 12:1–5) that Mary gave birth to became her Savior *and* the Savior of the world.

If you are a Christian, the story of Mary and Gabriel has likely been re-enacted in your life.

Perhaps you remember the day a preacher (man of God), or some other person invited you to accept Jesus—and you accepted Him. Then maybe you remember a subtle change beginning in your life. You were becoming more kind to others. Your peace of mind grew. You became aware of a Spiritual Presence watching over you. Then you *realized* that Jesus was with you and you were His disciple. It became your utmost desire to please Him in everything you did—like a newlywed man or woman desires to please his or her spouse. You were in love with Jesus. And you *knew* Jesus loved you.

Paul the Apostle, introduced Christ to the Corinthian church (see 1 Corinthians 4:15). Later, Paul became worried that the Corinthians were losing their devotion to Jesus—their Heavenly Husband:

> *For I am jealous over you with godly jealousy: for I have espoused you to one husband, that I may present you as a chaste virgin to Christ. ³ But I fear, lest by any means, as the serpent beguiled Eve through his subtilty, so your minds should be corrupted from the simplicity that is in Christ.* (2 Corinthians 11:2–3)

Paul, a man of God, was much like Gabriel, the man of God. He was an emissary who brought the Gospel message of betrothal to a "woman"—the Corinthian church (see Ephesians 5:23–23 and 31–32).

The apostle Paul was afraid that the Corinthian betrothal to Jesus was being interrupted by the Wicked Angel—Satan (see 2 Corinthians 11:13–15). After all, Paul had taught them well about family devotion and the virginal purity that unmarried women should maintain:

> *But he that is married careth for the things that are of the world, how he may please his wife.* ³⁴ **There is difference also between a wife and a virgin. The unmarried woman careth for the things of the Lord, that she may be holy both in body and in spirit**: *but she that is married careth for the things of the world, how she may please her husband.* (1 Corinthians 7:33–34)

The Corinthian church had drifted off the straight path that Paul had given them by his teaching and by his own personal example. They allowed people who had sex outside the holy matrimony of marriage to remain in the congregation:

> *I can hardly believe the report about the sexual immorality going on among you—something that even pagans don't do. I am told that a man in your church is living in sin with his stepmother. ² You are so proud of yourselves, but you should be mourning in sorrow and shame. And you should remove this man from your fellowship.* (1 Corinthians 5:1–2 NLT)

The Apostle delayed visiting their church on his missionary travels—to give them time to purge the sin and the sinners out of the assembly:

> *Now I call upon God as my witness that I am telling the truth. The reason I didn't return to Corinth was to spare*

> *you from a severe rebuke. * ²⁴ *But that does not mean we want to dominate you by telling you how to put your faith into practice. We want to work together with you so you will be full of joy, for it is by your own faith that you stand firm.* (2 Corinthians 1:23–24 NLT)

> *For I am afraid that when I come I won't like what I find, and you won't like my response. I am afraid that I will find quarreling, jealousy, anger, selfishness, slander, gossip, arrogance, and disorderly behavior. * ²¹ *Yes, I am afraid that when I come again, God will humble me in your presence. And I will be grieved because many of you have not given up your old sins.* **You have not repented of your impurity, sexual immorality, and eagerness for lustful pleasure.** (2 Corinthians 12:20–21 NLT)

If you are spiritual, then you know that Paul's words in the verses above are the Words of Jesus for the Corinthian church *and* for contemporary churches. In these modern times, the word *virgin* has become a dirty word—unless one is preaching about the Virgin Mary. **Paul prescribed the marriage bed as a remedy for sexual desire:**

> *Now regarding the questions you asked in your letter. Yes, it is good to live a celibate life. * ² *But* **because there is so much sexual immorality, each man should have his own wife, and each woman should have her own husband.** ³ *The husband should fulfill his wife's sexual needs, and the wife should fulfill her husband's needs. * ⁴ *The wife gives authority over her body to her husband, and the husband gives authority over his body to his wife. * ⁵ *Do not deprive each other of sexual relations, unless you both agree to refrain from sexual intimacy for a limited time so you can give yourselves more completely to prayer. Afterward, you*

should come together again so that Satan won't be able to tempt you because of your lack of self-control. (1 Corinthians 7:1–5 NLT)

Thousands of girls and young women attend church each week in this country. And thousands of Sunday school lessons are taught and thousands of sermons are preached. But I have yet to hear one lesson or sermon (other than in our church) about 1 Corinthians 7:34:

There is difference also between a wife and a virgin. The unmarried woman careth for the things of the Lord, that she may be holy both in body and in spirit.

Christian girls and boys are not being taught that Jesus expects them to be virgins when they marry. A multitude of preachers are making a lot of noise about the subject of abortion—but they are strangely silent on the subject of virginity. The virginally quiet pulpiteers are all the more puzzling—when one considers the fact that the Gospel of Jesus Christ began with a young woman who was a virgin.

It is the duty of every Christian (not just women and girls)—as a member of the Bride and Wife of Christ (see Ephesians 5:30–32)—to be inwardly and outwardly the kind of person that Jesus would marry—if He were walking the earth today. All Christians should "reflect the glory of the Man"—Jesus.

The woman [Church] is the glory of the man [Jesus]. (1 Corinthians 11:7)

Scripture teaches us that every Christian marriage should *mirror* the marriage between Christ and the Church:

For a husband is the head of his wife as Christ is the head of the church. He is the Savior of his body, the church. [24] *As* *the church submits to Christ, so you wives should submit to your husbands in everything. ²⁵ **For husbands, this means love your wives, just as Christ loved the church.** He gave up his life for her ²⁶ to make her holy and clean, washed by the cleansing of God's word. ²⁷ He did this to present her to himself as a glorious church without a spot or wrinkle or any other blemish. Instead, she will be holy and without fault. ²⁸ In the same way, husbands ought to love their wives as they love their own bodies. For a man who loves his wife actually shows love for himself. ²⁹ No one hates his own body but feeds and cares for it, just as Christ cares for the church. ³⁰ And we are members of his body. ³¹ As the Scriptures say, "A man leaves his father and mother and is joined to his wife, and the two are united into one."³² This is a great mystery, but **it is an illustration of the way Christ and the church are one.*** (Ephesians 5:23–32 NLT)

The Book of Esther is a spiritual play that portrays the story of Jesus the Bridegroom and the Church—His Bride. **It is the only book in the Bible that does not mention *God*, the *Lord*, *Jesus*, or the *Holy Spirit*.**

In the theatrical drama of Esther, King Ahasuerus (who ruled from India to Ethiopia: see Esther 1:1) represents Jesus. The seven wise men of the King represent the seven spirits of God (see Revelation 4:5). Esther represents the Bride of Christ. The proud and wicked Prime Minister Haman, who wanted to wipe out the Jewish race, represents the Devil (see Esther 3:5–13 and 7:6).

Like the virgin Esther, it must be your desire to make yourself as physically and as spiritually attractive as possible—so that King Jesus will choose you for his bride.

So it came to pass, when the king's commandment and his decree was heard, and when many maidens [many maid-

ens represent many different churches] were gathered together unto Shushan the palace, to the custody of Hegai, that Esther [Esther represents a humble and obedient church] was brought also unto the king's house, to the custody of Hegai [Hegai represents the Holy Spirit] keeper of the women. ⁹ *And the maiden pleased him, and she obtained kindness of him; and he speedily gave her things for purification, with such things as belonged to her, and seven maidens, which were meet to be given her, out of the king's house: and he preferred her and her maids unto the best place of the house of the women.* (Esther 2:8–9)

Now when the turn of Esther . . . was come to go in unto the king [Jesus], she required nothing but what Hegai [the Holy Spirit] the king's chamberlain, the keeper of the women, appointed. And Esther obtained favour in the sight of all them that looked upon her. ¹⁶ *So Esther was taken unto king Ahasuerus into his house royal in the tenth month, which is the month Tebeth, in the seventh year of his reign.* ¹⁷ *And the king loved Esther above all the women [the worldly churches and other religions in the world], and she obtained grace and favour in his sight more than all the virgins; so that he set the royal crown upon her head, and made her queen instead of Vashti [Vashti represents the Jews].* ¹⁸ *Then the king made a great feast [the great feast represents the Wedding Reception in Heaven] unto all his princes and his servants, even Esther's feast; and he made a release to the provinces, and gave gifts, according to the state of the king.* (Esther 2:15–18)

The humility, obedience, and the beauty of Esther caused the King to choose her as Queen and co-ruler of his kingdom. She is a prophecy of the time when the truly humble and obedient Church of Jesus will fulfil the following Scriptures:

> *And the king said unto Esther at the banquet of wine, What is thy petition? and it shall be granted thee: and what is thy request? even to the half of the kingdom it shall be performed.* (Esther 5:6)

> *Those* [churches] *who are victorious will sit with me on my throne, just as I was victorious and sat with my Father on his throne.* (Revelation 3:21 NLT)

> *Let us be glad and rejoice, and let us give honor to him. For the time has come for the wedding feast of the Lamb, and his bride has prepared herself. ⁸ She has been given the finest of pure white linen to wear. For the fine linen represents the good deeds of God's holy people. ⁹ And the angel said to me, "Write this: Blessed are those who are invited to the wedding feast of the Lamb." And he added, "These are true words that come from God."* (Revelation 19:7–9 NLT)

[4]

The Prophesy of Circumcision

This is my covenant, which ye shall keep, between me and you and thy seed after thee; every man child among you shall be circumcised.[11] *And ye shall circumcise the flesh of your foreskin; and it shall be a token of the covenant betwixt me and you . . .*[13] *He that is born in thy house, and he that is bought with thy money, must needs be circumcised: and my covenant shall be in your flesh for an everlasting covenant.*

Genesis 17:10–13

ABRAHAM IS THE FATHER OF circumcision. He was also a man of great faith. Before he was circumcised—when his wife Sarai (Sarah) was unable to conceive a child—he received a promise from God that his descendants would be as numerous as the stars in the night sky:

> *The Lord spoke to Abram [Abraham] in a vision and said to him, "Do not be afraid, Abram, for I will protect you, and your reward will be great."*[2] *But Abram replied, "O Sovereign Lord, what good are all your blessings when I don't*

> *even have a son? Since you've given me no children, Eliezer*
> *of Damascus, a servant in my household, will inherit all*
> *my wealth. ³ You have given me no descendants of my own,*
> *so one of my servants will be my heir." ⁴ Then the Lord said*
> *to him, "No, your servant will not be your heir, for you will*
> *have a son of your own who will be your heir." ⁵ Then the*
> *Lord took Abram outside and said to him, "Look up into*
> *the sky and count the stars if you can. That's how many*
> *descendants you will have!" ⁶ And Abram believed the Lord,*
> *and the Lord counted him as righteous because of his faith.*
> (Genesis 15:1–6 NLT)

Abraham is also the father of the Arabs and the Jews. And because of his faith, he is called the *father of our Christian faith*:

> *And Abraham is also the spiritual father of those who have*
> *been circumcised, but only if they have the same kind of*
> *faith Abraham had before he was circumcised. ¹³ Clearly,*
> *God's promise to give the whole earth to Abraham and his*
> *descendants was based not on his obedience to God's law,*
> *but on a right relationship with God that comes by faith . .*
> *. And we are all certain to receive it, whether or not we live*
> *according to the law of Moses, if we have faith like Abra-*
> *ham's. For <u>Abraham is the father of all who believe</u>.¹⁷ That*
> *is what the Scriptures mean when God told him, "I have*
> *made you the father of many nations."* (Romans 4:12–17
> NLT)

Abraham's original name was *Abram*, and his wife's original name was *Sarai*. He was seventy-five years old when God first said He would bless the earth through him. Abraham believed God, even though his wife was unable to have children.

By the time Abram was eighty-five years old, he had not had one child. That's when his wife planted an idea in his mind:

> *Now Sarai, Abram's wife, had not been able to bear chil-*
> *dren for him. But she had an Egyptian servant named*
> *Hagar. ² So Sarai said to Abram, "The Lord has prevented*
> *me from having children. Go and sleep with my servant.*
> *Perhaps I can have children through her." And Abram*
> *agreed with Sarai's proposal. ³ So Sarai, Abram's wife, took*
> *Hagar the Egyptian servant and gave her to Abram as a*
> *wife. (This happened ten years after Abram had settled in*
> *the land of Canaan.) ⁴ So Abram had sexual relations with*
> *Hagar, and she became pregnant. But when Hagar knew*
> *she was pregnant, she began to treat her mistress, Sarai,*
> *with contempt. (Genesis 16:1–4 NLT)*

This was the biggest mistake Abram made. It caused a loss of peace in his household:

> *Then Sarai said to Abram, "This is all your fault! I put my*
> *servant into your arms, but now that she's pregnant she*
> *treats me with contempt. The Lord will show who's wrong—*
> *you or me." ⁶ Abram replied, "Look, she is your servant, so*
> *deal with her as you see fit." Then Sarai treated Hagar so*
> *harshly that she finally ran away. (Genesis 16:5–6 NLT)*

> *The angel of the Lord found Hagar beside a spring of water*
> *in the wilderness, along the road to Shur. ⁸ The angel said*
> *to her, "Hagar, Sarai's servant, where have you come from,*
> *and where are you going?" "I'm running away from my*
> *mistress, Sarai," she replied.*

⁹ The angel of the Lord said to her, "Return to your mistress, and submit to her authority." ¹⁰ Then he added, "I will give you more descendants than you can count."

¹¹ And the angel also said, "You are now pregnant and will give birth to a son. You are to name him Ishmael (which means 'God hears'), for the Lord has heard your cry of distress. ¹² This son of yours will be a wild man, as untamed as a wild donkey! He will raise his fist against everyone, and everyone will be against him. Yes, he will live in open hostility against all his relatives." . . .

¹⁵ So Hagar gave Abram a son, and Abram named him Ishmael. ¹⁶ Abram was eighty-six years old when Ishmael was born. (Genesis 16:7–16 NLT)

When Hagar gave birth to Ishmael, the loss of peace continued in Abram's family (see Genesis 21:8–11). The bad situation was the result of his mistake of placing the word of his wife above the word of God (like Adam in the Garden of Eden: see Genesis 3: 17). Abram's error is evident in the loss of peace in the Middle Eastern world today. His misstep has given birth to wars and conflict between the nation of Israel (the descendants of Abraham and Sarah) and the Arab nations (the descendants of Abram and Hagar).

Ishmael became the father of the Arabians. The Arabians gave birth to the Islamic religion. And the Islamic religion has spawned a legion of suicide bombers who love death and martyrdom.

Ishmael's birth was because of Sarai's *human* attempt to bring about the fulfilment of God's promise. The minds of Sarai, Abram, and Hagar conspired together to produce Abram a son for God. The sex organs and the sex desire of Abram and Hagar were in a sense co-conspirators of Sarai's plot. Ultimately the plot backfired and failed—but an evil man and subsequently an evil religion was born into the world by means of their human action.

Ishmael was born *before* Abram was circumcised. **When God finally gave Abraham a child through Sarah—Isaac was born after the circumcision "ritual of the cutting off of the penis."**

> *When Abram was ninety-nine years old, the Lord appeared to him and said, "I am El-Shaddai—'God Almighty.' Serve me faithfully and live a blameless life.*[2] *I will make a covenant with you, by which I will guarantee to give you countless descendants."*

> [3] *At this, Abram fell face down on the ground. Then God said to him,* [4] *"This is my covenant with you: I will make you the father of a multitude of nations!* [5] *What's more, I am changing your name. It will no longer be Abram. Instead, you will be called Abraham, for you will be the father of many nations.*[6] *I will make you extremely fruitful. Your descendants will become many nations, and kings will be among them!*

> [7] *"I will confirm my covenant with you and your descendants after you, from generation to generation. This is the everlasting covenant: I will always be your God and the God of your descendants after you.*[8] *And I will give the entire land of Canaan, where you now live as a foreigner, to you and your descendants. It will be their possession forever, and I will be their God."*

> [9] *Then God said to Abraham, "Your responsibility is to obey the terms of the covenant. You and all your descendants have this continual responsibility.*[10] *This is the covenant that you and your descendants must keep: Each*

male among you must be circumcised.11 You must cut off
the flesh of your foreskin as a sign of the covenant between
me and you.12 From generation to generation, every male
child must be circumcised on the eighth day after his birth.
This applies not only to members of your family but also to
the servants born in your household and the foreign-born
servants whom you have purchased.[13] All must be circumcised. *Your bodies will bear the mark of my everlasting cov-*
enant.[14] Any male who fails to be circumcised will be cut off
from the covenant family for breaking the covenant."

[15] Then God said to Abraham, "Regarding Sarai, your
wife—her name will no longer be Sarai. From now on her
name will be Sarah. [16] And I will bless her and give you a
son from her! Yes, I will bless her richly, and she will become the mother of many nations. Kings of nations will be
among her descendants."

[17] Then Abraham bowed down to the ground, but he laughed
to himself in disbelief. "How could I become a father at the
age of 100?" he thought. "And how can Sarah have a baby
when she is ninety years old?"[18] So Abraham said to God,
"May Ishmael live under your special blessing!"

[19] But God replied, "No—Sarah, your wife, will give birth
to a son for you. You will name him Isaac, and I will con-
firm my covenant with him and his descendants as an everlasting covenant.[20] As for Ishmael, I will bless him also,
just as you have asked. I will make him extremely fruitful
and multiply his descendants. He will become the father of
twelve princes, and I will make him a great nation.[21] But
my covenant will be confirmed with Isaac, who will be born

to you and Sarah about this time next year." ²² *When God had finished speaking, he left Abraham.*

²³ *On that very day Abraham took his son, Ishmael, and every male in his household, including those born there and those he had bought. Then he circumcised them, cutting off their foreskins, just as God had told him.* ²⁴ *Abraham was ninety-nine years old when he was circumcised, 25 and Ishmael, his son, was thirteen.* (Genesis 17:1–25 NLT)

Abraham's son Isaac (not Ismael), was the son that was promised by God's Word. He was born *after* Abraham was circumcised. His birth after circumcision was a prophetic sign that he was born according to the will of God. It was a sign that his birth wasn't simply a matter of human desire and human sexual activity. John 1:13 in the New Testament perfectly applies to the birth of Isaac:

[Sons] *Which were born, not of blood, nor of the will of the flesh, nor of the will of man, but of God.*

Circumcision speaks of keeping the commandment of God to be fruitful and multiply by filing the earth with *children born only according to the will of God.*

Circumcision, as a ritual of the cutting off of the penis—*is a prophetic revelation of the original sin.* It is a declaration that the sin that caused Adam and Eve to cover their sexual anatomy will one day be reversed.

The events in the lives of Abraham and Sarah are a prophetic retelling of the events in the lives of Adam and Eve. Both Adam and Abraham are founding fathers. Adam is the father of mankind, and Abraham is the father of faith. They both placed the word of their wives above the Word of God (see Genesis 3:17 and 16:2). By their mistakes, they both caused a loss of peace on earth. And they both caused an evil son to be born into the world—Cain: Eve's son, and Ishmael: Hagar's son.

This is probably the first time anyone has asked you this question about Cain: **Why did the first human sex act give birth to Cain—an evil murderer who lied to God?** (Genesis 4:8–10) That question is a profound question. It's thought provoking. You won't find it in Sunday school publications anywhere in the world. The answer to this question seems like a mystery—but it's not. The answer is actually simple: *Cain was born because of Eve's Serpent-inspired sex act—instead of waiting on God and God designed Immaculate Conception.* **That's why Eve was *cursed* to have bloody and painful childbirths** (and bloody menstrual periods: see Genesis 3:16).

I will further explain the question above, and how it relates to circumcision. The answer lies in the understanding of Deuteronomy 32:8 (NLT):

> *When the Most High* [God] *assigned lands to the nations, when he divided up the human race, he established the boundaries of the peoples according to the number in his heavenly court.* [As in Dead Sea Scrolls, which reads: the number of the sons of God, and the Greek version, which reads: the number of the angels of God.]

God created you and me and every human born (according to His will) on earth with a corresponding angel in heaven. Jesus said the same thing in Matthew 18:10–11:

> *Take heed that ye despise not one of these little ones; for I say unto you, That in heaven their angels do always behold the face of my Father which is in heaven.* [11] *For the Son of man is come to save that which was lost.*

Your "angel" in heaven is the God-created divine part of your being. But the correspondence between you and your *angelic twin* was lost by your sex-initiated birth in flesh. Every human born since the fall of mankind has been born without access to God's celestial world. Hence, you were born a "lost soul."

> *For I was born a sinner—yes, from the moment my mother conceived me.* (Psalm 51:5 NLT)

The sexless birth of Jesus is a reversal of the curse of sex. Jesus has the power "seek and to save all who are lost." Jesus, as the Last Adam (see 1 Corinthians 15:45–47), has the power to cause you to be "born again" with the angelic spirit that God created for you before the world was formed.

> *Jesus answered and said unto him, Verily, verily, I say unto thee, Except a man be born again, he cannot see the kingdom of God.* (John 3:3)

To be *born again* means to be "born from above" in the original Greek language of the New Testament. There are some people that will never be "born from above" because they were born into the world via Satan-inspired sex and lust. The apostle Paul calls these people in Romans 9:22 *"vessels of wrath fitted to destruction."* Peter describes them in 2 Peter 2:12 *"as natural brute beasts, made to be taken and destroyed."* This category of human beings—the people of destruction—is also described in the book of Psalms:

> *The wicked are estranged from the womb: they go astray as soon as they be born, speaking lies.* (Psalm 58:3)

Jesus, in His parable of the "wheat and the weeds," explains how two classes of people got into the world. In His parable, Jesus reveals that there are only two races of people in the world—the people of the kingdom of God, and the people of the "evil one" (the Devil). In explaining this parable, Jesus reveals that the good seeds (wheat) are people that were placed on earth by God—and the bad seeds (weeds) are people who were *inserted* in the world by the Devil:

> Jesus replied, "The Son of Man is the farmer who plants the good seed. [38] The field is the world, and the good seed represents the people of the Kingdom. The weeds are the people who belong to the evil one. [39] The enemy who planted the weeds among the wheat is the devil. The harvest is the end of the world, and the harvesters are the angels. [40] "Just as the weeds are sorted out and burned in the fire, so it will be at the end of the world. [41] The Son of Man will send his angels, and they will remove from his Kingdom everything that causes sin and all who do evil. [42] And the angels will throw them into the fiery furnace, where there will be weeping and gnashing of teeth. [43] Then the righteous will shine like the sun in their Father's Kingdom. Anyone with ears to hear should listen and understand! (Matthew 13:37–43 NLT)

Before teaching the parable of the wheat and the weeds, Jesus declared that the purpose of his parables was to *reveal the secrets of the Kingdom of Heaven to His disciples*—while hiding the heavenly mysteries from the world at large:

> His disciples came and asked him, "Why do you use parables when you talk to the people?" [11] He replied, "You are permitted to understand the secrets of the Kingdom of Heaven, but others are not. [12] To those who listen to my teaching, more understanding will be given, and they will have an abundance of knowledge. But for those who are not

listening, even what little understanding they have will be taken away from them.[13] *That is why I use these parables, For they look, but they don't really see. They hear, but they don't really listen or understand.* (Matthew 13:10–13 NLT)

Jesus always used stories and illustrations like these when speaking to the crowds. In fact, he never spoke to them without using such parables. [35] *This fulfilled what God had spoken through the prophet: "I will speak to you in parables. I will explain things hidden since the creation of the world.* (Matthew 13:34–35 NLT)

The parable of the wheat and the weeds also explains the prophecy of circumcision. The "good seed" are people born according to God's predestinated will. The "bad seed" are people born because of human will and human sexual activity.

In the Great Tribulation period of the last days, Satan will incarnate in a man called the *Beast.* Everyone in the world will worship the Beast-man except one category of people—those whose names are in the Book of Life from before the creation of the world.

*And all the people who belong to this world worshiped the beast. They are the ones **whose names were not written in the Book of Life** before the world was made—the Book that belongs to the Lamb who was slaughtered.* (Revelation 13:8 NLT)

The "Book of Life before the world was made" is *God's record of the spirits of all people that would eventually be born on the earth.* The book that Revelation 13:8 speaks of is the register of the children of God mentioned in Deuteronomy 32:8. It is also the record of the angels that Jesus speaks of in Matthew 18:10.

Cain, the evil man born because of Eve's Serpent-inspired sex act, is not in God's angelic Book of Life. That is why he could receive an evil spirit from Satan at the dawn of the human race. His birth, and the understanding of the prophecy of circumcision, adds more clarity to this Scripture:

> *The wicked are estranged from the womb: they go astray as*
> *soon as they be born, speaking lies.* (Psalm 58:3 KJV)

Cain (and Ishmael) were born without a spiritual record in the Book of Life of Predestinated Births (see Romans 8:29–30)—births that were to occur on earth at the proper time—according to the will of God.

God wants His children born on earth according to His will and direction. If people are born on earth outside of His divine guidance, the destruction of peace that follow will be devastating. Cain and Ishmael are examples of children born from parents in an "uncircumcised state."

Sex outside of the holy matrimony of God's providence is devastating the lives of people inside and outside the church. Much of the poverty among Christian people is because they have cheapened their bodies with cheap sex (see Proverbs 21:17).

The doctrine of the prophecy circumcision will be hard for many church people to grasp because they have cheapened their minds with *cheap religion*. It is rare to find a preacher who preaches *more* than the basics of Hebrews 6:1–2 (NLT):

> *So let us stop going over the basic teachings about Christ*
> *again and again. Let us go on instead and become mature*
> *in our understanding. Surely we don't need to start again*
> *with the fundamental importance of repenting from evil*
> *deeds and placing our faith in God.* [2] *You don't need further*

*instruction about baptisms, the laying on of hands, the res-
urrection of the dead, and eternal judgment.*

Sunday after Sunday, week after week, month after month, and
year after year, many church members are fed a watered down version of Hebrews 6:1–2. <u>Their ability to think spiritually is retarded
from a biblical diet that is lacking in diversity, depth, and insight</u>.
They get stuck on the infantile level that Hebrews 5:12–13 explains:

> *For when for the time ye ought to be teachers, ye have need
> that one teach you again which be the first principles of
> the oracles of God; and are become such as have need of
> milk, and not of strong meat.* [13] *For every one that useth
> milk is unskilful in the word of righteousness: for he is a
> babe.* (Hebrews 5:12–13)

Jesus spoke of ministers that take away the key of knowledge
from people:

> *"What sorrow awaits you experts in religious law! For you
> remove the key to knowledge from the people. You don't en-
> ter the Kingdom yourselves, and you prevent others from
> entering."* (Luke 11:52 NLT)

<u>The key to Bible knowledge is still being taken away from people
by preachers</u>. It happens when the preachers emphasize the same
Scriptures (like John 3:16 and John 3:3) over and over again. It happens when lazy preachers preach from books of sermons that were
written by other preachers for other people. It happens when preachers preach using the calendar—emphasizing birthdays and holi-
days—instead of God's Holy Day. And it happens when preachers
emphasize music and entertainment—*instead of the knowledge of God's
word.*

Away with your noisy hymns of praise! I will not listen to the music of your harps. ²⁴ *Instead, I want to see a mighty flood of justice, an endless river of righteous living.* (Amos 5:23–24 NLT)

My people are destroyed for lack of knowledge: because thou hast rejected knowledge, I will also reject thee, that thou shalt be no priest to me: seeing thou hast forgotten the law of thy God, I will also forget thy children. (Hosea 4:6)

www.ingramcontent.com/pod-product-compliance
Lightning Source LLC
Chambersburg PA
CBHW060610030426
42337CB00018B/3023